P9-DMO-496

MAYA

Big Buddy Books

An Imprint of Abdo Publishing
www.abdopublishing.com

Sarah Tieck

www.abdopublishing.com

Published by Abdo Publishing, a division of ABDO, PO Box 398166, Minneapolis, Minnesota 55439. Copyright © 2015 by Abdo Consulting Group, Inc. International copyrights reserved in all countries. No part of this book may be reproduced in any form without written permission from the publisher. Big Buddy Books™ is a trademark and logo of Abdo Publishing.

Printed in the United States of America, North Mankato, Minnesota.
102014
012015

THIS BOOK CONTAINS
RECYCLED MATERIALS

Cover Photo: © J Marshall - Tribaleye Images/Alamy; Shutterstock.com.
Interior Photos: ©Al Argueta/Alamy (p. 13); © blickwinkel/Alamy (p. 29); Yvette Cardozo (p. 16); *Getty Images*: Chip HIRES/Contributor (p. 30); Glowimages.com (pp. 15, 17, 21, 27); ©Michele and Tom Grimm/Alamy (p. 13); © Heritage Image Partnership Ltd/Alamy (p. 9) © iStockphoto.com (pp. 19, 25, 26); © J Marshall - Tribaleye Images/Alamy (p. 11); © John Mitchell/Alamy (pp. 5, 17), © North Wind Picture Archives (p. 25); © travelstock.ca/Alamy (p. 23).

Coordinating Series Editor: Rochelle Baltzer
Contributing Editors: Bridget O'Brien, Marcia Zappa
Graphic Design: Adam Craven

Library of Congress Cataloging-in-Publication Data

Tieck, Sarah, 1976-
  Maya / Sarah Tieck.
     pages cm. -- (Native Americans)
  ISBN 978-1-62403-581-4
  1. Mayas--Juvenile literature. I. Title.
  F1435.T54 2015
  972.81--dc23
                        2014028400

CONTENTS

AMAZING PEOPLE

Thousands of years ago, North America was mostly wild, open land. Native American tribes lived on the land. They had their own languages and **customs**.

The Maya (MEYE-uh) are one Native American group. They are known for their powerful kings and skilled builders. They built one of the world's greatest **civilizations**. Let's learn more about these Native Americans.

Did You Know?

The name *Maya* comes from an ancient city named Mayapán. It was once an important center of Mayan power and culture.

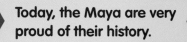

Today, the Maya are very proud of their history.

Maya Territory

Maya homelands were in Mexico and Central America. This area is known as Mesoamerica.

Mayans lived on the Yucatan **Peninsula** in Mexico. They also lived in Guatemala, Belize, Honduras, and El Salvador. These places have beaches, jungles, and mountains.

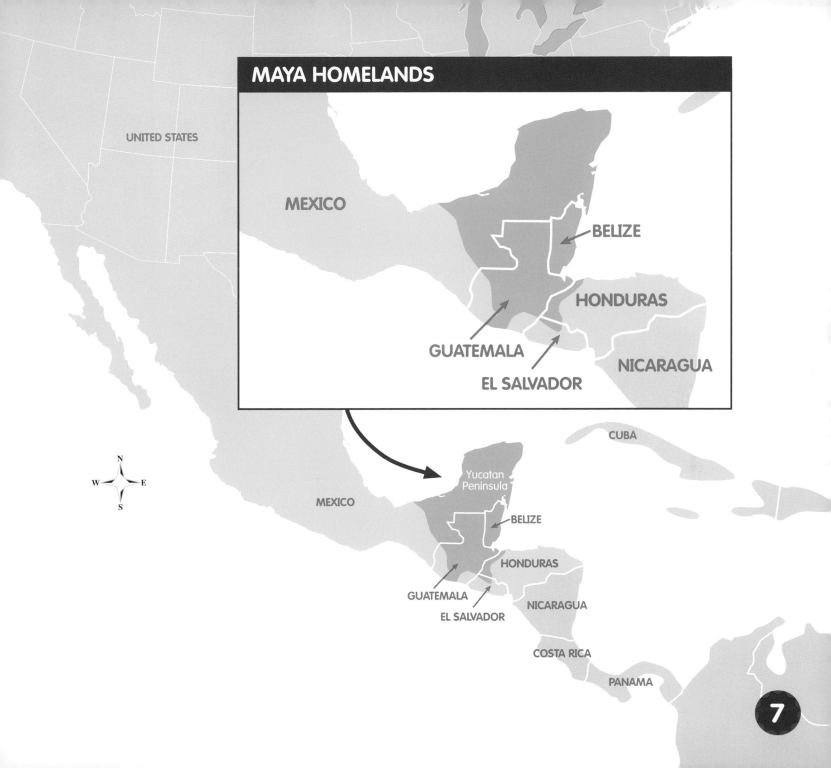

MAYA HOMELANDS

UNITED STATES

MEXICO

BELIZE

HONDURAS

GUATEMALA

EL SALVADOR

NICARAGUA

CUBA

Yucatan Peninsula

MEXICO

BELIZE

HONDURAS

GUATEMALA

EL SALVADOR

NICARAGUA

COSTA RICA

PANAMA

N
W   E
S

HOME LIFE

Most Mayan families lived in homes built from wood, stone, and mud. The floors were covered with soil. Wood poles supported mud walls. Palms covered the roof. Wealthier families lived in homes made of mostly stone.

People often think of great Mayan cities with buildings made of limestone. But, most people lived in simpler homes. They were made from materials found in jungles.

WHAT THEY ATE

The Maya were skilled farmers. They farmed corn, or maize. They also grew vegetables, such as beans and squash.

The Maya turned these foods into tortillas, tamales, and other meals. They grew extra food to save and to sell at markets.

The Maya practiced slash-and-burn farming. This means they used fire to clear land for crops.

Daily Life

The Maya first lived in villages. Later, they built large cities. At the peak of Mayan **civilization**, a city could have more than 20,000 people.

In ancient times, Mayan women wore long, loose dresses. Men wore simple cloths to cover their lower bodies. Upper-class Mayans wore decorated clothes and bright feather headdresses. They also wore jade and shell jewelry.

Mayan clothing has changed over the years. Today, some men wear bright colors and hats.

Mayan women are known for being skilled weavers. They make colorful cloth for many uses, including clothing.

Mayan people had different jobs. Men hunted, fished, and farmed. They were warriors, builders, artists, priests, and kings. Being powerful was important to Mayan men. Women took care of the children and ran the homes. They got water and firewood. They made food. There were no schools. So, children learned by helping and watching others in the community.

Today, some Mayan women still cook foods over open flame.

Made by Hand

The Maya made many objects by hand. They often used natural materials. These arts and crafts added beauty to everyday life.

Musical Instruments

Music and dance were important to the Maya. The people made drums, rattles (*right*), and wind instruments, such as flutes. These were used in some religious ceremonies.

Carvings and Pottery

Mayans carved jade (*left*) and wood. They also painted images on pottery. Their carvings and paintings told stories about their history and life.

Stone Stelae

The Maya made tall sculptures to honor their kings. Known as stelae (STEE-lee), they were covered in carvings. One of the largest known today is Stela E (*right*). It is 35 feet (11 m) tall and weighs 65 tons (59 tonnes).

Painted Murals

Mayans painted the walls of their homes and other buildings. These paintings showed daily life, religious rituals, and famous battles.

SPIRIT LIFE

Mayan religion was based on nature. **Ceremonies** honored gods and goddesses of the sun, moon, rain, and corn. The Maya built temples and pyramids for them.

One Mayan **ritual** was the Mayan Ball Game. Players fought to shoot a ball through a hoop. Kings and priests watched them play in a court. Some losers were **sacrificed**.

Did You Know?

Mayan pyramids were built to carry sound. This helped leaders easily talk to large groups of people.

El Castillo is a famous pyramid in the Mayan city of Chichén Itzá. It was made to show the movement of the sun. Many ceremonies were held there.

STORYTELLERS

The Maya told stories to pass on their **culture**. They shared stories about how their people fit into the world. Stories were sometimes acted out.

Mayans are famous for creating a written language. It is made of **hieroglyphs**. The Maya used hieroglyphs in books, paintings, and art.

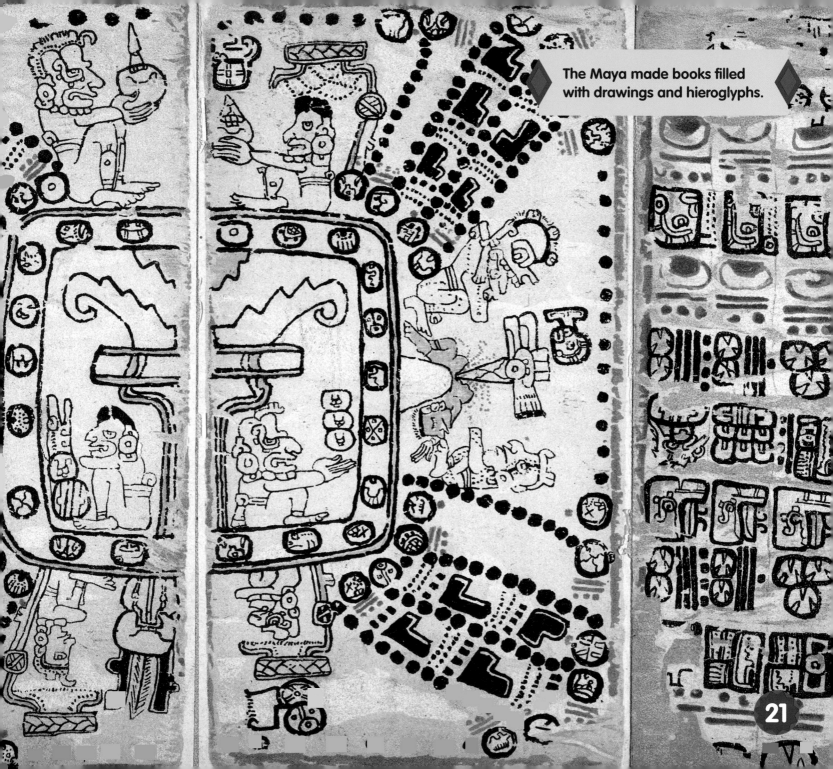

The Maya made books filled with drawings and hieroglyphs.

21

A STRONG CIVILIZATION

Around 2000 BC, the Mayan **civilization** began in Guatemala with small settlements. Later, the Maya built cities with stone pyramids and temples. They mapped the movement of the sun, stars, and planets.

The Maya reached their peak between 250 and 900 AD. There were many cities. Some famous Mayan cities were Tikal (tee-KAHL), Copán (koh-PAHN), and Palenque (pah-LEHN-kay).

The Maya painted records of their history and their kings.

Mayan **culture** became strong. Much of it came from the Olmec, who lived before the Maya. The Maya made art, played music, and had an advanced math system. Their **civilization** was one of the most powerful of its time.

By 900, the Mayan civilization had begun to **decline**. This continued for many years. The Spanish arrived around 1517. Before long, they took control of the Maya. Over time, Mayan ways of life changed to reflect the Spanish.

Did You Know?

The Maya made a 365-day calendar that repeats every 52 years.

Mayan buildings in Chichén Itzá were influenced by the Toltec. These people became powerful in Central Mexico about 900.

The Spanish changed life for the Maya. They tried to change their religion, and they destroyed their writings.

BACK IN TIME

600-400 BC

The Mayans built their first large pyramids.

About 900

Chichén Itzá became the most powerful Mayan city in its area. It was the ruling city until around 1200.

1519

Hernán Cortés and his men arrived in Mexico. They brought diseases that killed many Maya.

1962

Many Mayan **hieroglyphs** were recorded in a book. People worked to understand Mayan writing.

About 1830

People began to seriously explore Mayan sites and learn about their **culture**.

1979

The ruins of the city of Tikal were named a UNESCO Heritage Site.

THE MAYA TODAY

The Maya have a long, rich history. They are remembered for their carved calendars and written language. Today, the Maya live in Mexico, Guatemala, and Belize.

Mayan roots run deep. The people have kept alive those special things that make them Maya. Even though times have changed, many people carry the **traditions**, stories, and memories of the past into the present.

Did You Know?

Today, there are about 7 million Mayans living in Mexico and Central America.

Today, Mayan kids carry on culture and traditions.

"The struggle we fight purifies and shapes the future. Our history is a living history, that has throbbed, withstood and survived many centuries of sacrifice. Now it comes forward again with strength. The seeds, dormant for such a long time, break out today with some uncertainty . . ."

— Rigoberta Menchú Tum,

Nobel Peace Prize winner and activist

GLOSSARY

ceremony a formal event on a special occasion.

civilization a well-organized and advanced society.

culture (KUHL-chuhr) the arts, beliefs, and ways of life of a group of people.

custom a practice that has been around a long time and is common to a group or a place.

decline to slowly lose strength and value.

hieroglyph (heye-uh-ruh-GLIHF) a picture that represents an idea or a sound.

peninsula land that sticks out into water and is connected to a larger piece of land.

ritual (RIH-chuh-wuhl) a formal act or set of acts that is repeated.

sacrifice a person or animal killed as an offering to please a god.

tradition (truh-DIH-shuhn) a belief, a custom, or a story handed down from older people to younger people.

WEBSITES

To learn more about Native Americans, visit **booklinks.abdopublishing.com**. These links are routinely monitored and updated to provide the most current information available.

INDEX